Heart Power Safety Signal

Welcome!

We are glad you are here! These Safetypowers Safety Signals will help you to create a common language with the children, teens, and adults in your life about what it means to be safe with your bodies, your feelings, and your relationships with others.

Learning, teaching, and practicing these simple gestures, drawings, and words together helps people of all ages and abilities to remember to use these skills and follow these safety rules everywhere they go, in-person and online.

At Kidpower Teenpower Fullpower International, we have been teaching and sharing our Safety Signals as part of our programs with families, schools, organizations, and communities worldwide for many years.

In the first section of this book, the **Safety Signals Charts** show how to group the skills and safety rules in order to help us:

- Prevent and stop trouble with people
- Stay safe with our feelings, words, and bodies
- Build better relationships
- Take charge of our safety out in public
- Develop healthy boundaries with people we know
- Take charge of our feelings

In the second section, **Using Safety Signals In Daily Life** provides cartoon-illustrated examples showing children, youth, and adults using the skills to prevent and solve different kinds of problems with people.

The third section provides **Individual Safety Signals** with one drawing per page so that you can easily show, copy, and post the ones that are most important for members of your family or your students to remember and use.

You can also find downloadable overviews of our Safety Signals in English, Spanish, French, and adapted for New Zealand at **Kidpower.org/safetysignals.**

Please contact us at safety@kidpower.org to tell us how you are using this book and to share any suggestions. We look forward to hearing from you!

Table of Contents

Safety Signal Charts — 4
Prevent and Stop Trouble with People 5
Stay Safe with Our Feelings, Words, and Bodies 6
Build Better Relationships 7
Take Charge of Our Safety in Public 8
Understand, Set, and Respect Boundaries 9
Take Charge of Our Feelings 10

Using Safety Signals in Daily Life — 11
Prevent and Stop Trouble with People 12
Stay Safe with Our Feelings, Words, and Bodies 13
Build Better Relationships 14
Take Charge of Our Safety Out in Public 15
Understand, Set, and Respect Boundaries 16
Take Charge of Our Feelings 17

Introduction to Individual Safety Signals — 18

Prevent and Stop Trouble with People
Calm Down Power 19
Mouth Closed Power 20
Hands and Feet Down Power 21
Hang On Power 22
Speak Up Power 23
Fence Power 24
Trash Can Power 25
Heart Power 26

Stay Safe with Our Feelings, Words, and Bodies
Wait Power 27
Awareness Power 28
Stay Together Power 29
Check First Power 30
Think First Power 31
Walk Away Power 32
Roll Away Power 33
Get Help Power 34

Build Better Relationships
Listening Power 35
Speak Up Power 36
No, Thank You Power 37

Connection Power 38
Appreciation Power (Hooray Power!) 39
Make A Bridge Power 40
Make A Fence Power 41
Make A Wall Power 42

Take Charge of Our Safety in Public
Awareness Power 43
Voice Power 44
Look Away Power 45
Stop Power 46
Walk Away Power (Alternative version) 47
Move Away Power 48
Get Help Power (Find Safety) 49
Persistence Power 50

Understand, Set, and Respect Boundaries
We Each Belong To Ourselves 51
Some Things Are Not a Choice 52
Problems Should Not Be Secrets 53
Keep Telling Until You Get Help 54
Safe 55
Allowed by the Adults in Charge 56
Not a Secret, So Others Can Know 57
Choice of Each Person 58

Take Charge of Our Feelings
Stay in Touch With Our Emotions 59
Feelings 60
Be Assertive 60
Be Grateful 61
Be Courageous 62
Be Confident 63
Use Our 'Eyes of Love' 64
Use Our 'Emotional Raincoat' 65
Use Our 'Emotional Safety Screen' 66

Online Kidpower Resources 67
Acknowledgments 68
About Our Author 69
About Our Illustrator 69
Copyright and Permission To Use Information 71

Safety Signal Charts

Trash Can Power Safety Signal

The Safetypowers program shows how we can use our many kinds of POWER to stay SAFE.

These Safetypowers help us to prevent harm such as bullying, abuse, and violence - and to develop positive relationships that reduce isolation, protect mental health, and increase happiness.

The following Safety Signals Charts are grouped so you can see how the Safetypowers skills and safety rules that these signals represent fit together to prepare ourselves and others to:

- Prevent and stop trouble with people
- Stay safe with our feelings, words, and bodies
- Build better relationships
- Take charge of our safety out in public
- Develop healthy boundaries with people we know
- Take charge of our feelings

These charts make it easy to teach the Safety Signals and then do practices using the Safetypowers shown. We have often seen students of different ages and abilities using the charts to teach each other.

For your personal use, you have permission to enlarge, print, and post up to 10 copies of each of these copyrighted charts for teaching your own family, classroom, clients, or group. You can request permission to make additional print copies by emailing us at safety@kidpower.org You can tell people to visit Kidpower.org/safetysignals to download their own charts in English, Spanish, French, and adapted for Pacifica cultures.

safetypowers SAFETY SIGNALS
Prevent and Stop Trouble with People

The keys to remembering to use 'People Safety' strategies and skills in real life are simplicity, repetition, consistency, fun, and practice

Wait Power
Hold your own hands to help you stay safe, patient, and respectful when you need to wait - even though you want to say, do, or have something.

Awareness Power
Point towards your head. Use your whole body to stay aware of what is happening both inside you and around you. Notice what you see, smell, hear, touch, taste, and feel. Turn your body to show that you are paying attention to what is around you.

Stay Together Power
Start with your palms apart and facing outwards, and then move them together to remind yourself to Stay Together to stay safe out in public.

Check First Power
Gently clasp your forearm with the other hand to remind yourself to Check First with the adults who care about you before you change your plan about where you are going, who is with you, and what you are doing.

Think First Power
Pat your head gently to remind yourself to Think First about what to do when the unexpected happens or when someone is acting unsafely.

Walk Away Power
Walk in place with your feet to remind yourself to Walk Away from trouble and get to Safety.

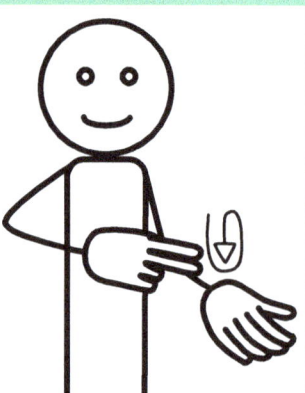

Roll Away Power
Roll your fingers along your arm to remind yourself to use wheels, such as a bike, car, or wheelchair to Roll Away from trouble and get to Safety.

Get Help Power
Put your arms in front of you with palms facing up to remind yourself to reach out to others to Get Help or to make a connection.

safetypowers® SAFETY SIGNALS
Stay Safe with Our Feelings, Words, and Bodies

Safety Signals are simple gestures, drawings, and words to help all of us remember important 'People Safety' ideas and skills

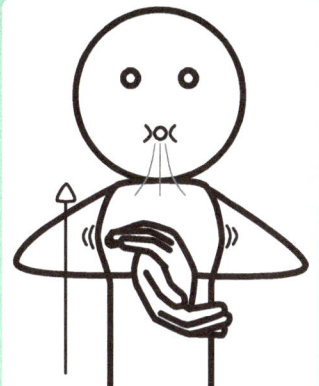

Calm Down Power
Press your palms together, straighten your back, breathe deeply and slowly, and feel your feet on the ground to help yourself Calm Down if you are scared or angry.

Mouth Closed Power
Squeeze your lips together to help you remember that you can stop yourself from saying something hurtful or doing something unsafe with your mouth.

Hands and Feet Down Power
Put your arms down to your sides and your feet firmly on the ground to remind you to stop yourself from bothering or hurting someone with your hands or feet.

Hang On Power
If you have a hard time stopping yourself from touching, grabbing, throwing, pushing or hitting someone or something you should not, hang onto your legs, pants, or shirt to help you stay in charge of your body.

Speak Up Power
Put your hand in front of your mouth and move it outwards to remind yourself to Speak Up about what you do and do not want.

Fence Power
Put your hands in front of your waist with your palms facing downwards. This helps you remember to set a boundary by letting someone know that you want them to stop bothering you.

Trash Can Power
Put a hand on your hip and pretend the hole it makes is your personal trash can. Use your other hand to catch hurting words and throw them away to remind you to protect yourself against hurtful words.

Heart Power
Reach forward and then press your hands into your chest to remind yourself to scoop kind words into your heart, protect your heart, and use your heart to be kind to others.

A publication of Kidpower Teenpower Fullpower International® www.kidpower.org For permission to copy, contact safety@kidpower.org

safetypowers SAFETY SIGNALS
Build Better Relationships
We can have more fun and fewer problems
with people when we use these Safety Powers

Listening Power
Put one hand behind your ear to remind yourself that Listening to others helps you learn and understand.

Speak Up Power
Put your hand in front of your mouth and move it outwards to remind yourself to Speak Up about what you do and do not want.

'No, Thank You' Power
Put your hand up, palm out, and shake your head "No" to remind yourself that even if you really like someone, you can say, "No, thank you!" to anything that makes you or others less safe.

Connection Power
Clasp your fingers together firmly in front of your body. This helps you remember that, in order to stay connected with people we care about, we need to hang on tightly.

Appreciation Power (Hooray Power!)
Shake your hands in the air or clap your hands with enthusiasm to remind yourself that when we cheer for people, we are letting them know that we appreciate them.

Make a Bridge Power
Put your hands in front of your body waist-high with your palms facing upwards to remind yourself to reach out to others if you need help or want to join an activity.

Make a Fence Power
Put your hands in front of your waist with your palms facing downwards. This helps you remember to set a boundary by letting someone know that you want them to stop bothering you.

Make a Wall Power
Put your hands in front of your chest with your palms facing outwards. This helps you remember to protect yourself if someone is acting unsafely by making a clear barrier between your body and that person.

safetypowers SAFETY SIGNALS
Take Charge of Our Safety in Public

If someone is acting in a way that feels unsafe,
we can make safer choices using these Safety Powers

Move Away Power
Put your hands in front of you with your palms facing each other. Suppose one hand is a person acting unsafely and the other hand is you. Move that hand away from the other to remind yourself that you can Move Away from trouble.

Voice Power
Use a loud and powerful voice to get attention from others to get help or to stop someone who is trying to scare or hurt you.

Look Away Power
Turn your head to the side or down and Look Away rather than staring at someone and making them uncomfortable. You can also use Look Away Power to stop yourself from looking at something unsafe for you.

Stop Power
Make your hands like a wall and say, "STOP!". This can help you let someone know that you want them to stop doing something unsafe, disrespectful, or harmful.

Walk Away Power (Alternative version)
Walk your fingers like two little legs along your arm to remind yourself to Walk Away from trouble and get to Safety.

Roll Away Power
Roll your fingers along your arm to remind yourself that you can use wheels, such as a bike, car, or wheelchair, to Roll Away from trouble and get to Safety.

Get Help Power (Find Safety)
Put your hands out in front of you with your palms facing up to remind yourself to go to Safety and reach out to someone in order to Get Help.

Persistence Power
Put your hands a few inches apart facing each other about shoulder high. Move them back and forth to remind yourself to be persistent, keep going, and not give up when you need help or are setting a boundary.

safetypowers® SAFETY SIGNALS
Understand, Set, and Respect Boundaries

These Safety Signals help everyone, everywhere remember the boundary rules and principles for staying safe and having fun with people we know

Safety Signals for The Four Kidpower Boundary Rules

We each belong to ourselves
Point to yourself, sit or stand tall, and smile to remind yourself that each person's body, time, feelings, and thoughts are important.

Some things are not a choice
Shrug and smile to remind yourself that some things are required, and boundaries often have to be negotiated, even for adults.

Problems should not be secrets
Hold a finger in front of your mouth. Move the finger away from your mouth to remind yourself that we are safer when we can talk about our problems.

Keep telling until you get help
Have one hand say, 'I need help.' and the other hand reply, 'I will help you.' to remind yourself to tell until you get help.

Safety Signals for the Kidpower Consent Checklist:
Touch, relationships, or activities should be SAFE, ALLOWED by the adults in charge, and not have to be secret, so OTHERS CAN KNOW.

Safe
Hug yourself to remind yourself that we all deserve to be and feel safe.

Allowed by the adults in charge
Curl your hand and pretend it's the head of and adult in charge nodding "Yes". Touch, play, and affection need to be allowed by the adult in charge.

Not a secret, so others can know
Open your hands and raise both arms above your head to remind yourself that touch, play, and affection should not have to be a secret.

The choice of each person
Put two thumbs up to remind yourself that each person needs to agree about touch, attention, and games for play, affection, and fun.

A publication of Kidpower Teenpower Fullpower International®   www.kidpower.org   For permission to copy, contact safety@kidpower.org

safety powers® SAFETY SIGNALS
Take Charge of Our Feelings

Stay in Touch with Your Emotions
Put one hand over your heart and notice the warmth of your skin, the beating of your heart, and what you are feeling at that moment. Paying attention to your emotions can help you to stay safe.

Be Assertive
Put your pointer finger into the air and give a little smile. Speaking up in ways that are powerful, clear, and respectful can help you to get someone's attention and have them listen to what you want to say.

Be Grateful
Put your elbows down near your sides and turn the palms of your hands up. Connect with something you are grateful for and say or think, "Thank you!". Gratitude helps you to focus on the good things in your life, in our world, in others, and in yourself.

Be Courageous
Put your hands on your hips and imagine your heart being strong and brave. It often takes courage to do what you think is right and to take good care of the well-being of yourself and others.

Be Confident
Give yourself a pat on the back and think or say, "I believe in myself!". This can encourage you to Be Confident when facing challenges or when you are feeling nervous about doing something or talking with someone.

Use Your 'Eyes of Love'
Imagine that you are looking with love through your eyes and using your heart to see others with love, rather than getting upset with them about things they might not be able to change. You can also shape your hands into a heart and look through it.

Use Your 'Emotional Raincoat'
Think about how a raincoat helps keep your body warm and dry in a rainstorm. Now, imagine wearing an Emotional Raincoat to help your mind and body stay calm and peaceful when someone is yelling at you.

Use Your 'Emotional Safety Screen'
A screen on a window or door lets in the fresh air and keeps out the bugs. Criss-cross your fingers to make an Emotional Safety Screen. This can help you to screen out negativity or insults and take in useful information in order to figure out what to do.

Using Safety Signals in Daily Life

Stop Power Safety Signal

The following cartoon-illustrated pages provide examples of children, youth, and adults using their Safetypowers skills and safety rules to prevent and solve different kinds of problems with people.

You can use these examples to create your own examples and practices. Topics include how to:

- Prevent and stop trouble with people
- Being safe with our feelings, words, and bodies
- Build better relationships
- Take charge of our safety out in public
- Develop healthy boundaries with people we know

We have many more social stories and practices in our *Safety Comics series including* our Kidpower Children's Safety Comics, our Kidpower Youth Safety Comics, our Fullpower Safety Comics for Teens and Adults, and Girlpower: Be Confident for young women.

Prevent and Stop Trouble with People

When their friend gets angry and throws things, Aly uses their **Walk Away Power** and goes to play with another friend until their friend is feeling better.

Clara's and Sunny's neighbor invites them to come over. They have been at his house before, but they remember to use **Check First Power** before they change their plan.

"Your mom says you can come over to my house for cookies!"

"We'd love to, but we need to Check First with Mom ourselves."

Mei Lin uses **Think First Power** to be safe when meeting strangers.

A: I live near you and go to the same gym as you!

He is still a stranger. I'll check with my mom about how to meet him in a safer way if I decide to.

Stay Safe with Our Feelings, Words, and Bodies

Amelia's friend is in a bad mood and calls her "Stupid!". She uses her **Trash Can Power** to throw the word "Stupid" away.

Alva uses her **Speak Up Power** to protect her feelings when her friends make jokes about her freckles.

> Stop! I know you think it is a funny joke and I do not like it when peope make fun of my freckles.

 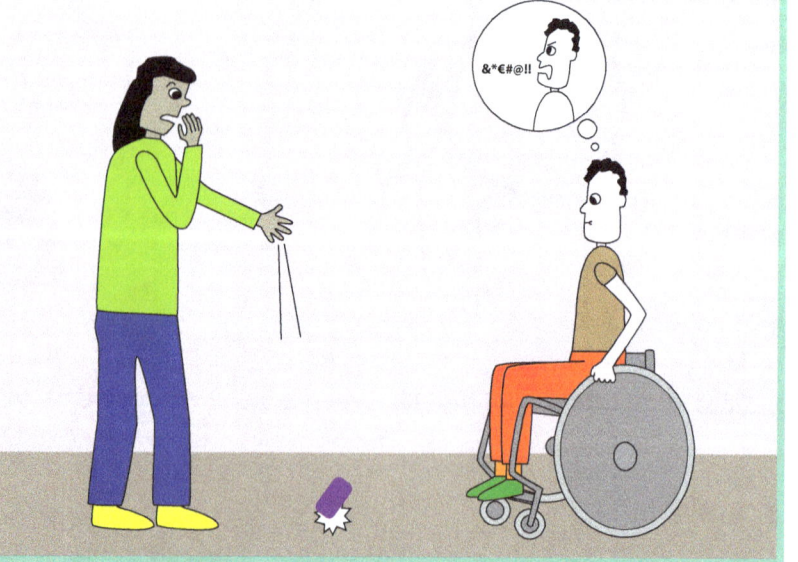

Mike gets upset when his friend drop's Mike's phone on the ground. Mike uses his **Mouth Closed Power** to avoid saying something mean to his friend because everyone can make mistakes.

Build Better Relationships

Stuarts likes giving his big sister hugs and kisses. When she says "no" to a kiss, he gets upset. But then he remembers his Listening Power and respects his sister's boundaries.

Armand sees his classmate sitting alone and looking sad. He decides to use his Connection Power and goes up to him to talk.

Mike keeps asking Rosa if she wants a back rub. She uses her Fence Power to tell him that she wants him to stop asking.

Taking Charge of Our Safety Out in Public

When Amita see's a stranger with her kitten, she uses her **Get Help Power** and goes inside to fetch her adult in charge to help her.

Emmet uses his **Voice Power** when he sees other people being unsafe - even though he feels embarrassed, he yells as loud as he can for help.

Some friends are at the mall. When two people they don't know start harassing them they use their **Move Away Power** to go to safety and get help.

14   A publication of Kidpower Teenpower Fullpower International®   www.kidpower.org   For permission to copy, contact safety@kidpower.org

Understand, Set, and Respect Boundaries

Anna and Carlos like to tickle. Carlos changes his mind and tells Anna to stop. Since touch for play should be the choice of each person, Anna listens and stops tickling Carlos.

Peter's friend Adam want to play a game that is *not* safe. So Peter sets a boundary and says, "No" - and suggests another game that is both fun *and* safe.

Talib and Mara are holding hands and only focused on each other in class. This is *not* allowed by the adult in charge. So they quickly let go and listen to the teacher.

Take Charge of Our Feelings

Use your **Emotional Safety Screen** to stay calm and make wise choices for yourself - instead of giving into someone - or creating a fight.

Be Courageous by persisting in speaking up for the rights, safety, and well-being of yourself and others.

When someone is gossiping and spreading rumors to make trouble between people you can use **your 'Eyes of Love'** to be kind and keep your heart open about others.

Introduction to Individual Safety Signals

Calm Down Power Safety Signal

Many people like to have full-page versions of the individual Safety Signals to use in teaching and to post as reminders.

Having one drawing per page makes it easy to show, copy, and post the Safety Signals that are most important for the people in your life to learn, remember, and use.

For your personal use, you have permission to make up to 30 copies a year of each of Individual Safety Signals for teaching your own family, classroom, clients, or group. You can request permission to make additional print copies by emailing us at safety@kidpower.org.

You can tell people to visit Kidpower.org/safetysignals to download the Safety Signals Charts in English, Spanish, French, and adapted for Pacifica cultures.

We also show how to teach the Safety Signals in our Online Learning Center including our Safetypowers course; our Starting Strong, Confident Kids, and Teenpower Classroom Lessons; our 8 Skills to Stop Bullying course, and our Safety Signals course.

safetypowers: Take Charge of Our Feelings, Words, and Bodies
Calm Down Power

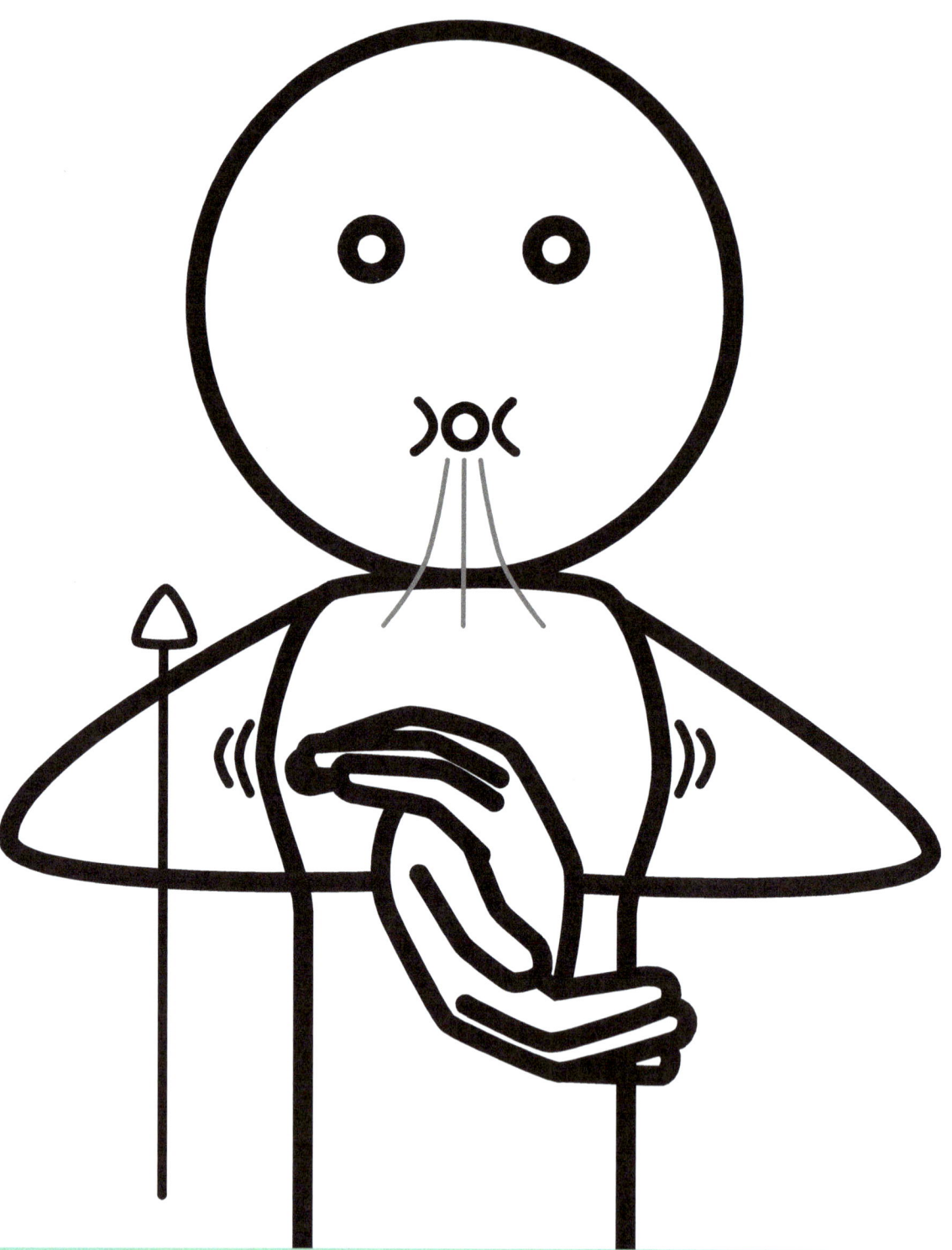

Press your palms together, straighten your back, breathe deeply and slowly, and feel your feet on the ground to help yourself Calm Down if you are scared or angry.

safetypowers Take Charge of Our Feelings, Words, and Bodies
Mouth Closed Power

Squeeze your lips together to help you remember that you can stop yourself from saying something hurtful or doing something unsafe with your mouth.

safetypowers **Take Charge of Our Feelings, Words, and Bodies**
Hands and Feet Down Power

Put your arms down to your sides and your feet firmly on the ground to remind you to stop yourself from bothering or hurting someone with your hands or feet.

safetypowers: Take Charge of Our Feelings, Words, and Bodies
Hang On Power

If you have a hard time stopping yourself from touching, grabbing, throwing, pushing or hitting someone or something you should not, hang onto your legs, pants, or shirt to help you stay in charge of your body.

safetypowers: Take Charge of Our Feelings, Words, and Bodies
Speak Up Power

Put your hand in front of your mouth and move it outwards to remind yourself to Speak Up about what you do and do not want.

safetypowers — Take Charge of Our Feelings, Words, and Bodies
Fence Power

Put your hands in front of your waist with your palms facing downwards. This helps you remember to set a boundary by letting someone know that you want them to stop bothering you.

safety powers: Take Charge of Our Feelings, Words, and Bodies
Trash Can Power

Put a hand on your hip and pretend the hole it makes is your personal trash can. Use your other hand to catch hurting words and throw them away to remind you to protect yourself against hurtful words.

safetypowers — Take Charge of Our Feelings, Words, and Bodies
Heart Power

Reach forward and then press your hands into your chest to remind yourself to scoop kind words into your heart, protect your heart, and use your heart to be kind to others.

safetypowers Help Prevent and Solve Problems
Wait Power

Hold your own hands to help you stay safe, patient, and respectful when you need to wait - even though you want to say, do, or have something.

safetypowers® Help Prevent and Solve Problems
Awareness Power

Point towards your head. Use your whole body to stay aware of what is happening both inside you and around you. Notice what you see, smell, hear, touch, taste, and feel. Turn your body to show that you are paying attention to what is around you.

safetypowers Help Prevent and Solve Problems
Stay Together Power

Start with your palms apart and facing outwards, and then move them together to remind yourself to Stay Together to stay safe out in public.

safetypowers Help Prevent and Solve Problems
Check First Power

Gently clasp your forearm with the other hand to remind yourself to Check First with the adults who care about you before you change your plan about where you are going, who is with you, and what you are doing.

safetypowers Help Prevent and Solve Problems
Think First Power

Pat your head gently to remind yourself to Think First about what to do when the unexpected happens or when someone is acting unsafely.

safetypowers Help Prevent and Solve Problems
Walk Away Power

Walk in place with your feet to remind yourself to Walk Away from trouble and get to Safety.

safetypowers Help Prevent and Solve Problems
Roll Away Power

Roll your fingers along your arm to remind yourself to use wheels, such as a bike, car, or wheelchair to Roll Away from trouble and get to Safety.

safetypowers Help Prevent and Solve Problems
Get Help Power

Put your arms in front of you with palms facing up to remind yourself to reach out to others to Get Help or to make a connection.

safetypowers Build Better Relationships
Listening Power

Put one hand behind your ear to remind yourself that Listening to others helps you learn and understand.

safetypowers Build Better Relationships
Speak Up Power

Put your hand in front of your mouth and move it outwards to remind yourself to Speak Up about what you do and do not want.

safetypowers Build Better Relationships
No, Thank You Power

Put your hand up, palm out, and shake your head "No" to remind yourself that even if you really like someone, you can say, "No, thank you!" to anything that makes you or others less safe.

safetypowers Build Better Relationships
Connection Power

Clasp your fingers together firmly in front of your body. This helps you remember that, in order to stay connected with people we care about, we need to hang on tightly.

safetypowers Build Better Relationships
Appreciation Power (Hooray Power!)

Shake your hands in the air or clap your hands with enthusiasm to remind yourself that when we cheer for people, we are letting them know that we appreciate them.

safetypowers Build Better Relationships
Make A Bridge Power

Put your hands in front of your body waist-high with your palms facing upwards to remind yourself to reach out to others if you need help or want to join an activity.

safetypowers Build Better Relationships
Make A Fence Power

Put your hands in front of your waist with your palms facing downwards. This helps you remember to set a boundary by letting someone know that you want them to stop bothering you.

safetypowers Build Better Relationships
Make A Wall Power

Put your hands in front of your chest with your palms facing outwards. This helps you remember to protect youself if someone is acting unsafely by making a clear barrier between your body and that person.

safetypowers Take Charge of Our Safety Out in Public
Move Away Power

Put your hands in front of you with your palms facing each other. Suppose one hand is a person acting unsafely and the other hand is you. Move that hand away from the other to remind yourself that you can Move Away from trouble.

safetypowers Take Charge of Our Safety Out in Public
Voice Power

Use a loud and powerful voice to get attention from others to get help or to stop someone who is trying to scare or hurt you.

safetypowers Take Charge of Our Safety Out in Public
Look Away Power

Turn your head to the side or down and Look Away rather than staring at someone and making them uncomfortable. You can also use Look Away Power to stop yourself from looking at something unsafe for you.

safetypowers — Take Charge of Our Safety Out in Public
Stop Power

Make your hands like a wall and say, "STOP!". This can help you let someone know that you want them to stop doing something unsafe, disrespectful, or harmful.

safety powers Take Charge of Our Safety Out in Public
Walk Away Power (Alternative version)

Walk your fingers like two little legs along your arm to remind yourself to Walk Away from trouble and get to Safety

safetypowers Take Charge of Our Safety Out in Public
Roll Away Power

Roll your fingers along your arm to remind yourself that you can use wheels, such as a bike, car, or wheelchair, to Roll Away from trouble and get to Safety.

safetypowers Take Charge of Our Safety Out in Public
Get Help Power (Find Safety)

Put your hands out in front of you with your palms facing up to remind yourself to go to Safety and reach out to someone in order to Get Help.

safetypowers Take Charge of Our Safety Out in Public
Persistence Power

Put your hands a few inches apart facing each other about shoulder high. Move them back and forth to remind yourself to be persistent, keep going, and not give up when you need help or are setting a boundary.

safetypowers Understand, Set, and Respect Boundaries
We Each Belong To Ourselves

Point to yourself, sit or stand tall, and smile to remind yourself that each person's body, time, feelings, and thoughts are important.

safetypowers Understand, Set, and Respect Boundaries
Some Things Are Not a Choice

Shrug and smile to remind yourself that some things are required, and boundaries often have to be negotiated, even for adults.

safetypowers Understand, Set, and Respect Boundaries
Problems Should Not Be Secrets

Hold a finger in front of your mouth. Move the finger away from your mouth to remind yourself that we are safer when we can talk about our problems.

safetypowers Understand, Set, and Respect Boundaries
Keep Telling Until You Get Help

Have one hand say, 'I need help.' and the other hand reply, 'I will help you.' to remind yourself to tell until you get help.

safetypowers Understand, Set, and Respect Boundaries
Safe

Hug yourself to remind yourself that we all deserve to be and feel safe.

safetypowers Understand, Set, and Respect Boundaries
Allowed by the Adults in Charge

Curl your hand and pretend it's the head of and adult in charge nodding "Yes". Touch, play, and affection need to be allowed by the adult in charge.

safetypowers Understand, Set, and Respect Boundaries
Not a Secret, So Others Can Know

Open your hands and raise both arms above your head to remind yourself that touch, play, and affection should not have to be a secret.

safetypowers Understand, Set, and Respect Boundaries
Choice of Each Person

Put two thumbs up to remind yourself that each person needs to agree about touch, attention, and games for play, affection, and fun.

safetypowers Take Charge of Our Feelings
Stay in Touch With Our Emotions

Put one hand over your heart and notice the warmth of your skin, the beating of your heart, and what you are feeling at that moment. Paying attention to your emotions can help you to stay safe.

safetypowers Take Charge of Our Feelings
Be Assertive

Put your pointer finger into the air and give a little smile. Speaking up in ways that are powerful, clear, and respectful can help you to get someone's attention and have them listen to what you want to say.

safetypowers Take Charge of Our Feelings
Be Grateful

Put your elbows down near your sides and turn the palms of your hands up. Connect with something you are grateful for and say or think, "Thank you!". Gratitude helps you to focus on the good things in your life, in our world, in others, and in yourself.

safetypowers Take Charge of Our Feelings
Be Courageous

Put your hands on your hips and imagine your heart being strong and brave. It often takes courage to do what you think is right and to take good care of the well-being of yourself and others.

safetypowers Take Charge of Our Feelings
Be Confident

Give yourself a pat on the back and think or say, "I believe in myself!". This can encourage you to Be Confident when facing challenges or when you are feeling nervous about doing something or talking with someone.

safetypowers Take Charge of Our Feelings
Use Our 'Eyes of Love'

Imagine that you are looking with love through your eyes and using your heart to see others with love, rather than getting upset with them about things they might not be able to change. You can also shape your hands into a heart and look through it.

safetypowers Take Charge of Our Feelings
Use Our 'Emotional Raincoat'

Think about how a raincoat helps keep your body warm and dry in a rainstorm. Now, imagine wearing an Emotional Raincoat to help your mind and body stay calm and peaceful when someone is yelling at you.

safetypowers' Take Charge of Our Feelings
Use the 'Screen Technique'

A screen on a window or door lets in the fresh air and keeps out the bugs. Criss-cross your fingers to make an Emotional Safety Screen. This can help you to screen out negativity or insults and take in useful information in order to figure out what to do.

EDUCATIONAL RESOURCES AND WORKSHOPS

Resource Library
kidpower.org/library

Newsletter
kidpower.org/newsletter

Downloads of ebooks, posters, & more
kidpower.org/downloads

Videos
kidpower.org/videos

Boundary & Consent Posters
kidpower.org/boundary-posters

Kidpower Coloring Book
kidpower.org/coloringbook

30 Skills Coaching Handbook
kidpower.org/30skills

Translated resources
kidpower.org/languages

Spanish Resources
kidpower.org/espanol

Online Learning Center
learn.kidpower.org/courses

Starting Strong Mini-Lessons
kidpower.org/minilessons

Safetypowers for People With Disabilities
kidpower.org/safetypowers

Full Circle Safety for K-12 Educators Sexual Abuse Prevention
kidpower.org/full-circle

Classroom Lessons
kidpower.org/k-12

Self-Defense Skills
kidpower.org/selfdefensecourse

Professional Development
kidpower.org/propower

Parents/Caregivers
kidpower.org/courses-for-parents

What We Do
kidpower.org/learnmore

Issues We Address
kidpower.org/issues

Who We Serve
kidpower.org/people

Live Online Workshops
kidpower.org/organize

Locations with local instuctors
kidpower.org/locations

Bullying Solutions
kidpower.org/bullying

Child Abuse Prevention
kidpower.org/abuse-prevention

Schools & Organizations
kidpower.org/schools

Prevention & Healing from Trauma
kidpower.org/mentalhealth

Kidpower Books from Preschool Years to University Years - kidpower.org/books

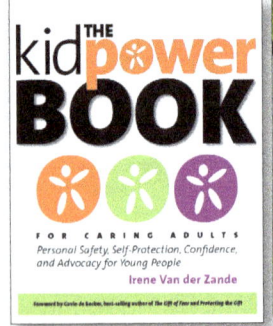

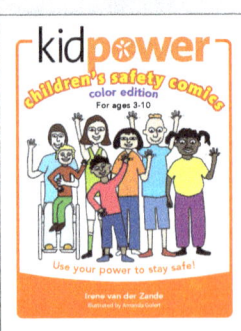
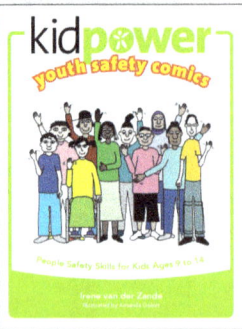
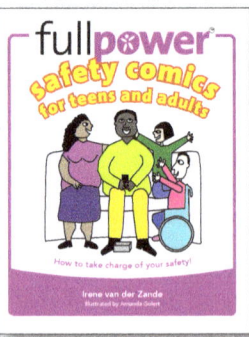

© A publication of Kidpower Teenpower Fullpower International® kidpower.org For permission to copy, contact safety@kidpower.org

Acknowledgments

Thank you to each of the remarkable people from around the world for your gifts of commitment, creativity, time, talent, and generosity!

Kidpower is a tapestry of many different threads woven by many different hands. Our curriculum and services have grown from the ideas, questions, teaching, feedback, and stories of countless people since I first started working on child protection, personal safety, and self-defense issues in 1985.

I want to express my appreciation to each of our Kidpower instructors, board members, honorary trustees, senior program leaders, center directors, workshop organizers, advisors, volunteers, donors, parents, students, funding partners, service partners, family members, advocates, hosts, and office staff.

Thank you for the thought, care, time, and generosity that you have given to bring Kidpower Teenpower Fullpower International to where we are today. I feel honored to have you as colleagues and as friends.

I want to give special acknowledgment to our Kidpower International Senior Program Leaders, who are highly experienced in teaching and/or organizing our programs and who have been with us for many years - and who have made significant contributions to the international organization as well as providing Kidpower services in their own communities. They include: Cornelia Baumgartner, Joe Connelly, Ellen Frankel, Amanda Golert, Angela Hamilton, Mary Jane Hayes, Jan Isaacs Henry, Zeina Hobeich, Meredith Henry, Ryan Holmes, Chantal Keeney, Marylaine Léger, Erika Leonard, John Luna-Sparks, Anne Mason, Beth McGreevy, Marc Meilleur, Amy Tiemann and Marìa Gisella Gámez.

Our Board of Directors includes the following deeply committed people who provide significant support to our organization: April Yee, Board President; Kim Leisey, Vice President; Peter Lewis, Treasurer; Penny Campbell Loftesness, Secretary; and members: Abby Bleistein, Claire Laughlin, Ellen Frankel, Dave Harrison, Arnie Kamrin, Rich Kamrin, Maryse Postelwaite, John Luna-Sparks, Jennifer Turner-Davis, Julie Shattuck, and Zaida Torres.

And, THANK YOU to Timothy Dunphy, who is our Kidpower International Program Co-Founder, for partnering with me in our early years to create our original programs that are the foundation of our work in ways that are effective, empowering, and FUN! – and for continuing to help bring Kidpower out into the world as a member of our training team.

Finally, I want to honor the memory of our long-time supporter, mentor, and former Board President Nancy Driscoll, whose wisdom and generosity have helped and keep helping Kidpower grow from a good idea into a great reality!

Take a look at our Annual Reports and History on our kidpower.org website to learn more about these people and the many other remarkable people who are working together to further Kidpower's vision of helping to create cultures of safety, respect, and kindness for everyone, everywhere.

Writing each person's story would be a book unto itself!

About Our Author

Irene van der Zande is the Founder and Executive Director of Kidpower Teenpower Fullpower International. Since 1989, Irene's talented leadership and collaboration have earned Kidpower an outstanding reputation worldwide for developing, organizing, and presenting high quality child protection, positive communication, advocacy, self-defense, and personal safety programs and curriculum for everyone, everywhere.

Irene is the co-author of the best-selling book, *Doing Right by Our Kids: Protecting Child Safety at All Levels*, which features Kidpower skills and principles as well as other best practices.

As Kidpower's expert lead author, Irene places time-tested life-saving social-emotional skills and lessons directly into the hands of parents and professionals through her numerous books, articles, and other educational resources.

She is an inspiring, passionate, and entertaining speaker, trainer, and storyteller who is a master at preparing people to transform problems into successful practices; to take charge of their safety and well-being; and to develop joyful relationships that enrich their lives.

About Our Illustrator

Amanda Golert is an experienced self-defense instructor, trainer, passionate advocate for personal safety for children and other vulnerable people, the Center Director of Kidpower Sweden—and she also likes to draw!

Since 1999, Amanda has supported the growth and development of Kidpower Teenpower Fullpower International. She works in partnership with Irene to illustrate, edit, and design the Kidpower cartoon books and many other educational materials.

In 2004, Irene was looking for someone who could draw the pictures she had in her head for our Kidpower curriculum - and she found Amanda! Since then, Amanda's keen eye, dry humor, skilled hands, and deep understanding of our work have led to our creation of educational materials that have helped millions of children, teens, and adults all over the world learn how to have more fun and fewer problems with people.

Thank You to Our Special Contributors

Trainer **John Luna-Sparks** was on our pilot team for teaching people with little or no speech and had the inspiration that led to these Safety Signals.

New Zealand Center Founder and Program Director **Cornelia Baumgartner** led the creation of developing Safety Signals for our Boundary and Consent Rules and the adaptations for Pacifica cultures.

Lebanon Center Director and Founder **Zeina Hobeich** led the creation of the Take Charge of Your Feelings Safety Signals and translated all of the Safety Signals into Arabic.

Stay connected!

Together, we can transform feelings of helplessness and despair into hope and confidence and greater safety for all. Join us.

Learn

Adding Kidpower skills to your life is easy! Use our Kidpower Starter Kit, for people of all ages and abilities, to protect and empower yourself and your loved ones:
kidpower.org/learnmore

Share

Share Kidpower with three important people in your life — such as friends, family, school, community, colleagues. Get and share new articles via our newsletter:
kidpower.org/newsletter

Give

Commit to making your community and the world a safer place by supporting Kidpower. We truly value all gifts of money, time, and expertise. Make your gift:
kidpower.org/donate

 /Kidpower.org

 /learn.kidpower.org

 /Kidpower.org

 /kidpowerintl

 /KidpowerIntl

 /company/Kidpower

 kidpower.org/volunteer/

 /Kidpower89

 safety@kidpower.org

Copyright and Permission To Use Information

Copyright Information
Safetypowers Safety Signals Book © 2023. All content in this book is copyrighted to author Irene van der Zande, Kidpower Teenpower Fullpower International founder and executive director. Except as indicated in the Reproduction Information below, no part of this publication may be shared or reproduced in any form or by any electronic or mechanical means, including information and retrieval systems, without prior written permission of the author or her designated representative.

Reproduction Information
This book includes special limited permission for the owner to make up to 10 print copies of the pages in the Safety Signals Charts section and up to 30 print copies a year of one or more of the pages in the Individual Safety Signals section for their personal use ONLY. Prior written permission for other people or other uses must be obtained before sharing or reproducing any part of this publication in any form. However, a wealth of resources including are available for free on www.kidpower.org. For information about how to obtain permission for different kinds of content, visit Kidpower.org/permission or contact the author or her authorized representative at safety@kidpower.org.

Use of Content for Personal Learning or for Teaching Others
With proper acknowledgment, readers are encouraged to use knowledge from the Kidpower Teenpower Fullpower programs about self-protection, confidence-building, advocacy, personal safety, positive communication, child protection, leadership, team-building, bullying prevention, child abuse prevention, positive youth development, and self-defense strategies and skills in their personal lives and professional activities.

We ask that readers tell people about Kidpower Teenpower Fullpower International when they use any examples, ideas, stories, language, and/or practices that they learned from our program, and let others know how to reach our organization.

Please note that permission to use content from our copyrighted programs verbally and in person is **not** permission to publish or duplicate any part of this content in any written or digital form in print or online, including in articles, lesson plans, research papers, videos, newsletters, books, videos, podcasts, websites, etc. These uses require separate permission as described above.

Restrictions
Unless people or agencies have an active agreement with Kidpower Teenpower Fullpower International, they are not authorized to represent themselves or give the appearance of representing themselves as working under our organization's auspices. This means that individuals and groups must have an active certification or agreement with our organization to be authorized to teach, promote, or organize workshops or other presentations using the Kidpower, Teenpower, Fullpower program names, workshop names, reputation, or credentials. Please visit www.kidpower.org or e-mail safety@kidpower.org about our instructor certification, authorized provider, and center development programs.

Liability Disclaimer
Each situation is unique, and we can make no guarantee about the safety or effectiveness of the content or techniques described in this material. We do not accept liability for any negative consequences from use of this material.

Kidpower Teenpower Fullpower International
Office: 831-2274723 or (USA) 1-800-467-6997
E-mail: safety@kidpower.org Web page: www.kidpower.org
Address: P.O. Box 1212, Santa Cruz, CA 95061, USA

www.ingramcontent.com/pod-product-compliance
Lightning Source LLC
LaVergne TN
LVHW081458060526
838201LV00057BA/3068